When God Weeps

Participant's Guide

Books by Joni Eareckson Tada

All God's Children: Ministry with Disabled Persons (with Gene Newman)

Barrier-Free Friendships: Bridging the Distance Between You and Friends with Disabilities (with Steve Jensen)

Diamonds in the Dust: 366 Sparkling Devotions

Heaven: Your Real Home

Heaven: Devotional Edition

Joni

The Life and Death Dilemma: Suicide, Euthanasia, Suffering, Mercy

More Precious Than Silver: 366 Daily Devotional Readings

A Step Further (with Steven Estes)

When God Weeps: Why Our Sufferings Matter to the Almighty (with Steven Estes)

When God Weeps

Why Our Sufferings Matter to the Almighty

Joni Eareckson Tada
Steven Estes

with Stephen and Amanda Sorenson

Participant's Guide

GRAND RAPIDS, MICHIGAN 49530 USA

We want to hear from you. Please send your comments about this book to us in care of the address below. Thank you.

GRAND RAPIDS, MICHIGAN 49530 USA
WWW.ZONDERVAN.COM

ZONDERVAN™

When God Weeps Participant's Guide
Copyright © 2002 by Joni Eareckson Tada and Steven Estes

Requests for information should be addressed to:

Zondervan, *Grand Rapids, Michigan 49530*

ISBN 0-310-24194-4

All Scripture quotations, unless otherwise indicated, are taken from the *Holy Bible: New International Version*®. NIV®. Copyright © 1973, 1978, 1984 by International Bible Society. Used by permission of Zondervan. All rights reserved.

All rights reserved. No part of this publication may be reproduced, stored in a retrieval system, or transmitted in any form or by any means—electronic, mechanical, photocopy, recording, or any other—except for brief quotations in printed reviews, without the prior permission of the publisher.

Published in association with the literary agency of Wolgemuth & Associates, Inc.

Interior design by Sherri L. Hoffman

Printed in the United States of America

03 04 05 06 07 08 /❖ DC/ 10 9 8 7 6 5 4 3 2

Contents

Preface 7

Session 1
A Good God in a Suffering World 9

Session 2
What Can Suffering Accomplish in Our Lives? 25

Session 3
How We Respond to Suffering Matters 43

Session 4
Jesus Gives Us Hope 61

Session 5
Finding Contentment 77

Session 6
A Look toward Heaven 99

Preface

A few years after I became paralyzed in a diving accident, I met Steve Estes. A mutual friend had introduced us and told me that Steve was really big into the Bible. So shortly after we met, I asked him the big question: "Tell me, do you think God had anything to do with my breaking my neck?"

That desperate, pain-laden question was all it took to set us on an adventure that continues to this day. During those early years, we spent hours journeying through Scripture together. We were determined to search out the God of the Bible and to know him as intimately as we could. I never dreamed that the truths I discovered then—and more important, my relationship with the God who stood behind them—would have such an impact on my life and on the lives of other suffering people.

As uncomfortable as it was at first, I learned that yes, God was in complete control the very moment I dove into the water and snapped my neck. But I also learned that he loved me no less then than he did before. With amazement, I learned that God would use whatever pain, suffering, or evil that came my way to warn me of the reality of hell, to make me long for a close relationship with him, to make me fit for life here and in the hereafter, and to woo me toward heaven. I learned how very much our afflictions touch the heart of God and how he uses them to touch our hearts.

Our desire through this Zondervan*Groupware*™ series is to share a portion of what we discovered with you. We want you to know that God truly weeps over human heartache. He feels our anguish, and his love drives him to allow us to suffer. We want to help you grow to know the God who longs to embrace us in his loving arms and to empower us to live with an unquenchable hope in the midst of our suffering.

We look forward to the day when "the eyes of the blind will be opened . . . and the lame shall leap like deer." We are anxious for all sorrow and pain to pass away. When it happens, we're sure we will marvel at how God worked it all for our good and his glory. Until that day, until God drops the curtain on suffering, we pray that we will trust in his love and commit our lives to the one who holds all the answers in his hands.

—Joni Eareckson Tada

Session One

A Good God in a Suffering World

Everyone who takes the Bible seriously, and many who don't, agree that God hates suffering.... But it simply doesn't follow that God's *only* relationship to suffering is to relieve it. —STEVE ESTES

Questions to Think About

1. Briefly describe a time when someone you love suffered. Explain how you felt, what you did for that person, how that experience affected your life, your beliefs, your faith in God, your actions.

   Was there anything you could have done to relieve that person's suffering but chose not to do? Why didn't you relieve the suffering? How did you feel about your decision?

2. How do you suppose God views our suffering? What does he feel? What does he do? What does he think?

3. What are some possible reasons a loving, good, and perfect God would allow suffering?

Session One: *A Good God in a Suffering World* • 11

Video Observations

Getting to know God in the midst of our suffering

Why a good, perfect, and sovereign God allows suffering

How God feels about suffering

Suffering can help us become more "God focused"

Video Highlights

1. What are some of the benefits of suffering that were mentioned in the video? How comfortable are you in considering these to be *benefits*?

2. What did you notice about Joni's attitude toward suffering?

3. What are your thoughts about Lamentations 3:32–33: "Though he [God] brings grief, he will show compassion, so great is his unfailing love. For he does not willingly bring affliction or grief to the children of men"?

4. Do you believe that people who are well acquainted with suffering often become closer to God as a result? Why or why not?

Large Group Exploration

How Do We Know That God Is Good, Loving, and Tender?

It's no secret that people, even Christians, suffer. But how can this be? Didn't God the Father send Jesus to release us from the bondage of sin and its effects? Doesn't God tell us to cast all our anxiety on him because he cares for us (1 Peter 5:7)? Doesn't he promise abundant life (John 10:10)? Doesn't he promise to give good gifts to his children (Luke 11:11–13)? Let's take a closer look at Scripture to see what we learn about this God we thought we knew. Let's see if we can reconcile who he is with the reality of human suffering.

1. Dozens of Scripture passages reveal that God is good. For a sampling of what Scripture says, look up the following descriptions of God's goodness.

Scripture	Description of God's Goodness
1 Chronicles 16:34	
Psalm 145:9	
Mark 10:18	
1 Peter 2:3	

> **JUST IN CASE YOU HAVE SOME DOUBTS . . .**
> In addition to the Scripture passages in question 1, you may want to read the following sampling of passages that affirm God's goodness and love: Ezra 3:11; Psalm 25:8; 34:8; 100:5; 106:1; 118:1; 135:3; Isaiah 63:7; Lamentations 3:25; Nahum 1:7.

2. With what expressions of tenderness does God describe his love for his people in Zechariah 2:8 and Zephaniah 3:17?

3. From the beginning through the end of Scripture, we read of God's great love for humankind and see the many ways in which he expresses that love. Read Micah 7:18–20, Ephesians 2:4–7, and 1 John 3:1. What does God's love lead him to do for us?

4. What does Jesus tell us about God's love in John 15:9–14?

5. Jesus, as God in human form, couldn't help but show God's love during his ministry on earth. Let's look at two snapshots of Jesus' life. How did he demonstrate God's love, compassion, and mercy?

   a. Mark 1:21–34

   b. John 11:32–36

Truth or Imagination?

What we think about God influences our friendship with him. It affects how much glory we give him. But our imaginations about God aren't reliable—ancient speculations about the kind of birthday present he might like led cultures into human sacrifice. Nor can we simply trust our emotions about him—if we conceive of God as we'd like him to be, we're sure to recreate him in our own image. We're liable to become like the people Paul described: "They are zealous for God, but their zeal is not based on knowledge" (Romans 10:2).

—STEVE ESTES

> ### ESSENTIAL BIBLICAL CONCEPT
> The one and only God exists as three persons—Father, Son, and Holy Spirit. The three of them are God together, drawing life and enjoyment from each other. We see particular evidence of this in Matthew 3:16–17, when Jesus was baptized and the Spirit descended on him and the Father in heaven expressed his pleasure with his Son.
>
> Because of the special relationship Jesus has with God the Father, they are fully united in thought and action (see Luke 10:22). As recorded in the gospel of John, Jesus said, "I and the Father are one" (John 10:30). In John 14:9–10, he explained to his disciples that because he and his Father are one, anyone who has seen him has seen the Father. Furthermore, anything Jesus said or did originated not just from him but from the Father as well. That is why Jesus is able to make the Father known to us (John 1:18).
>
> The New Testament writers understood this concept well. That is why Paul described Jesus as "the image of the invisible God" (Colossians 1:15) and the writer of Hebrews referred to Jesus as the "exact representation" of God's being (Hebrews 1:3).

6. It is one thing to know that God is love, but we need to know that we can count on God's love. What assurance of God's unfailing love do we find in 1 Samuel 15:29 and Hebrews 13:8?

Session One: *A Good God in a Suffering World* • 17

Small Group Exploration

Seeking to Know the Truth about God

When life is going well, most of us find it easy to believe that God is love and that he cares for us. But when we suffer pain, when tragedy strikes, or when we face troubles that don't go away, many of us begin to doubt what is true about God. We question if he loves us. We wonder if he really is in control. We wonder if he cares about our pain.

TOPIC A: Does God Really Control Our Suffering World?

This question plagues Christians and non-Christians alike. We wonder how it is possible for a loving and all-powerful God to be in control of a world in which so many bad things happen. We can't imagine how God can watch people endure great pain yet seem to do nothing about it. We may even wonder if he is powerless—or worse, malicious. Yet Scripture clearly indicates that God runs the world—all the time, even when we suffer. Let's explore this challenging perspective.

1. According to the following passages, what are some of the ways in which God controls what happens in the world?

    a. Amos 4:7–10

    b. Exodus 4:10–11

    c. Proverbs 16:4

2. Although people have the ability to make and are fully responsible for their decisions, God not only knows ahead of time what we will do but also directs our hearts to fulfill his plans. What does each of the following passages say about this?

   a. Psalm 139:1–4, 16

   b. Lamentations 3:37–38

   c. Psalm 33:11

   d. Proverbs 16:9; 19:21; 21:1

TOPIC B: Does God Really Care When People Suffer?

We know from the Gospels that Jesus felt great emotion as he ministered to people. His demonstrations of compassion help us know that God cares about our suffering, too. But long before Jesus came to earth, God showed his love and tender care for people who suffer. Look up the following verses and note how God the Father feels toward people who suffer and the ways in which he showed his concern for them.

Session One: A Good God in a Suffering World • 19

Scripture	God's Concern for People Who Suffer
Genesis 21:14–19	
Exodus 2:23–25; 3:7–10	
Leviticus 19:14	
1 Kings 17:20–24	
Psalm 34:17–18	
Psalm 116:1–9	
Isaiah 40:11	

Group Discussion

1. As you've read about God's love, his sovereign power, and his care for those who suffer, which new truths have you discovered? What do you see in a different light?

2. It's one thing to learn about who God is and what he does, but when we look around and consider the suffering that surrounds us—and even more when we suffer—it can be difficult to make sense out of it. How do you reconcile God's goodness with real life? Are you comfortable with what you know of God and life? If not, what troubles you?

3. If you have trouble reconciling a good God in control of a suffering world, consider for a moment the alternatives. What if, contrary to what the Bible claims, God is not the one who permits and screens all your sufferings? Then who does? Are you willing to say that ultimately your sufferings come only by chance? Or that Satan—not God—makes the ultimate decision about what trials your life will include?

Personal Journey: To Do Now

Spend a few minutes alone with God to consider the personal implications of God's loving character in relationship to suffering.

1. Write a short, personal summary of what your understanding of God's relationship to suffering was at the beginning of this session.

    a. What changes would you make in that summary as a result of what you have studied today?

    b. What further questions do you have as a result of what you discovered today?

2. What is your personal challenge in reconciling a loving God to the reality of suffering?

    a. What suffering do you think a good, loving God should not allow?

    b. What circumstances seem to fly in the face of what you know to be true of God?

> ## Faith in the Face of Suffering
>
> Faith is hard—God hides, says the Psalms. He plays his hand close to the vest; he never shows all the cards. "It is the glory of God to conceal a matter" (Proverbs 25:2). We can't see the good flowing from our heartaches. We may see some—perhaps we're a bit more patient since arthritis slowed us down—more sympathetic to single parents since our marriage collapsed.... But the good we can tally, does it outweigh the bad that we see? No. Eden's lost innocence opened sluice gates of sorrow deep beyond telling. It will take heaven to dry it all up—to provide the total picture that will ease our hearts forever. —STEVE ESTES

    c. Perhaps most important, what are you inclined to believe about God that isn't true?

3. In what ways has your suffering, or that of someone you love, positively or negatively affected your view of God? How can what you learned in this session strengthen your relationship with him?

Personal Journey: To Do on Your Own

During this session, we've started to discover more about the character of God and how he fulfills his purposes in a suffering world. We will learn more in the coming sessions, but we need much more than so-called "right answers." Our greatest need is for a deeper, more personal relationship with God. It is only through knowing and trusting him that we can find lasting peace in the midst of our suffering.

Set aside some time to do the following exercise.

1. Ask God to reveal to you any thoughts you have about him that may be hindering your ability to trust him and to receive the comfort and love he offers.

2. Take time to read and meditate on the following passages of Scripture, which focus on God's love and compassion: John 17:6–26, Zephaniah 3:14–20, and John 3:16–17.

A Glimpse of Suffering through the Eyes of God

God does look down on his world and weep. But its twistedness did not catch him by surprise. He knew that humans would fall into sin. He knew the immeasurable sorrow this would let loose. He knew the suffering it would cost his own Son. But he decreed to permit this fall because he knew how he would resolve it: that Jesus would die, that his church would eventually triumph through innumerable trials, that Satan's fingers would be pried off the planet, that justice would be served at the final judgment, that heaven would make up for all, and that God would receive more glory—and we would know more joy—than if the Fall had never happened. Can anyone but God see enough of this coming ecstasy to make sense out of our present agony? *God sees this glorious end as clearly as if it were today.*

—STEVE ESTES

Session Two

What Can Suffering Accomplish in Our Lives?

Unless the Bible is wrong, *nothing* happens outside of God's decree. Nothing good, nothing bad, nothing pleasant, nothing tragic. In simple language, God runs the world. Even when it sins. Even when we suffer. He permits others to do what he would never do. He has determined to steer what he hates to accomplish what he loves.   —STEVE ESTES

Questions to Think About

1. What goes through your mind when someone says, "I'm so glad I went through that time of pain or suffering because God has taught me so much through it"?

2. What examples can you give of when God used suffering to accomplish his purposes?

3. Take a brief inventory of your life so far and compare the ways in which you have grown during the difficult times with the ways in which you have grown during the easy times. What differences do you see?

Video Observations

What suffering can do

We will suffer

Suffering helps us see our need for God

Suffering empties us so God can fill us

Video Highlights

1. In the video, Joni describes her wheelchair as being a "huge blessing." What do you think enables Joni to consider her paralysis to be a blessing? What is your response to her perspective?

2. What are your initial thoughts as you consider the apostle Paul's plea to "join with me in suffering for the gospel, by the power of God" (2 Timothy 1:8)? Are you comfortable with the idea that we are called to suffer and that it is actually good for us? Why or why not?

3. As Lynn and Greg Linkowski shared about the suffering they have experienced, Greg concluded that "God is a most gracious and awesome God." How do you respond to that conclusion? Does it surprise you? Is it a conclusion you think you would have made? Why or why not?

4. Now that we have seen the video, let's make a list of some of the things we can learn and discover through times of suffering.

Large Group Exploration

God Allows What He Hates in Order to Accomplish What He Loves

The Bible records many incidents in which God steered evil—thoughts, decisions, and actions that are an affront to his holy character—in order to accomplish his work. Although God never tempts anyone (see James 1:13–17), he knows what is in everyone's heart and steers the evil that is already there so that it serves his good purposes. In *When God Weeps*, Steve Estes described God's actions this way: "It's as if he says, 'So you want to sin? Go ahead—but I'll make sure you sin in a way that ultimately furthers my ends even while you're shaking your fist in my face.'" The following Scripture passages will help us see how God works in this way without violating an individual's will.

1. In the following examples, describe the evil God allowed and note how it accomplished his good work.

    a. Samson's confrontations with the Philistines (See Judges 14:1–4; 15:1–8, 14–16; 16:23–30.)

    b. The Hebrews' departure from Egypt (See Exodus 10:24–28; 11:1, 9–10; 12:29–36; 14:5–9, 13–18.)

c. Joseph and his family (See Genesis 37:3–8, 19–20, 26–28; 45:4–8; 50:18–21.)

> **WHEN WE CAN'T SEE WHAT GOD IS DOING**
> As we, or those we love, face suffering, we try so hard to make sense out of our circumstances. When we can't come up with satisfactory answers, we often find ourselves questioning God. But our doubt is quite presumptuous. We seem to forget that we are dealing with the almighty God. Of course we cannot know what is happening behind the scenes! No one can grasp the Almighty. "Even angels long to look into these things.... Oh, the depth ... of the wisdom and knowledge of God! How unsearchable his judgments, and his paths beyond tracing out" (1 Peter 1:12; Romans 11:33).
>
> Just because we cannot comprehend God's work doesn't mean he isn't working. So when we face suffering and can't see a reason for it anywhere on the horizon, our best course is not to demand an answer from God or to presume that he is doing nothing on our behalf. Rather, we can choose to believe what God says is true: that he is at work to accomplish his ultimate, good purposes.

Small Group Exploration

PART 1: How Do We Know God Expects Us to Suffer?

Many Christians believe God doesn't want us to suffer. "Jesus healed people; he didn't make them suffer," they reason. They quote Isaiah 53, which says that we are healed by his wounds. They say Jesus has destroyed the devil's work and wants us to believe his promises so he can shatter the misery Satan creates and bring glory to himself. While these facts are true, the conclusion that God's people are to escape human suffering doesn't take into account the whole picture.

God wants to lavish us with everything that is good, wonderful, and glorious—we need look no farther than the Garden of Eden or through the gates of heaven to know that. But as Steve Estes noted in *When God Weeps*, "Eden's lost innocence opened sluice gates of sorrow deep beyond telling. It will take heaven to dry it all up—to provide the total picture that will ease our hearts forever." In the meantime, suffering is an inescapable part of life on earth, and those who follow Christ will suffer as they seek to accomplish God's work. Let's consider a few verses that shed light on our calling to suffer.

1. Do followers of Christ really have a calling to suffer? According to the following verses, what did Jesus and Paul have to say about this question?

    a. Luke 9:22–24

    b. Romans 8:12–17

A LEGACY OF SUFFERING FOR THE GOSPEL

What kind of suffering did the New Testament believers endure for the cause of Christ? Paul gives us an idea in 2 Corinthians 11:24–28:

> Five times I received from the Jews the forty lashes minus one. Three times I was beaten with rods, once I was stoned, three times I was shipwrecked, I spent a night and a day in the open sea, I have been constantly on the move. I have been in danger from rivers, in danger from bandits, in danger from my own countrymen, in danger from Gentiles; in danger in the city, in danger in the country, in danger at sea; and in danger from false brothers. I have labored and toiled and have often gone without sleep; I have known hunger and thirst and have often gone without food; I have been cold and naked. Besides everything else, I face daily the pressure of my concern for all the churches.

Many of the early believers suffered illness (Galatians 4:13; Philippians 2:25–27; 1 Timothy 5:23; 2 Timothy 4:20). Some, like Stephen, were killed (Acts 6:8–15; 7:54–60), and others were imprisoned (Acts 4:1–3). Christians scattered across Asia Minor suffered "grief in all kinds of trials" (1 Peter 1:6).

c. 2 Corinthians 1:5–7

d. Philippians 1:27–29

2. What does 1 Peter 4:12–13, 19 reveal about suffering and God's will?

PART 2: What Does Scripture Say about Suffering and Knowing God?

In the first chapter of *When God Weeps,* Joni proposed that suffering is a necessary part of our relationship with God. She referred to Philippians 3:10, where Paul responded to the Philippians' inquiry:

> "We want to be like you, Paul. What's your secret? How can we know God like you do?" The apostle confided to them in a letter. He described what fueled his remarkable spiritual life and what *he* craved:

> All I care for is to know Christ,
> to experience the power of his resurrection,
> and to share in his sufferings,
> in growing conformity with his death . . .
> Philippians 3:10 NEB

What? Becoming like Christ in his *death?* we ask. As in martyrdom by crucifixion? As in a living death where we "carry our cross" and God slowly wrenches from us everything we hold dear? You mean likeness to Christ's death as in being force-fed things I don't want while wanting things I don't have? Having suffering shoveled down my throat by God-who-says-he-loves-me? Ugh! . . . Who is this God who bids us crawl over broken glass just for the pleasure of his company?

1. Read Philippians 3:8–10.

    a. How much did Paul want to know Christ, and how great a price was he willing to pay for that privilege?

    b. Discuss the difference between Paul's approach to suffering and the approach Joni described above (which may be more like our own).

2. Joni wrote, "The invitation to know God—really know him—is always an invitation to suffer. Not to suffer alone, but to suffer with him." What do the following Scripture passages reveal about our unity with Christ and our participation in his suffering?

    a. Mark 8:34–35

    b. Hebrews 5:8–9

c. Romans 8:28–29

d. Matthew 10:21–24; Hebrews 4:14–15

The Beautiful Side of Suffering

God uses suffering to purge sin from our lives, strengthen our commitment to him, force us to depend on grace, bind us together with other believers, produce discernment, foster sensitivity, discipline our minds, spend our time wisely, stretch our hope, cause us to know Christ better, make us long for truth, lead us to repentance of sin, teach us to give thanks in times of sorrow, increase faith, and strengthen character. It is a *beautiful* image!

—JONI EARECKSON TADA

Group Discussion

1. As we've seen, suffering is much more than something bad that happens to us. How does our perception of suffering change when we consider it to be part of God's plan and calling for us, as part of sharing in something with Christ?

2. For most of us, it isn't easy to change our viewpoint and accept suffering for what God says it is rather than what it feels like it is. What have we discussed today that is hard for you to accept?

3. In *When God Weeps,* Steve Estes wrote, "Our call to suffer comes from a God tender beyond description. If we do not cling to this through life's worst, we will misread everything and grow to hate him." How important is it to believe in God's personal love and compassion for us when we face suffering?

4. Which things would you like to add to our list of what we learn and discover through our suffering? (See question 4 of Video Highlights.)

Personal Journey: To Do Now

Spend a few minutes alone with God to consider the role suffering plays in your life. Think about what God would have you learn about your suffering and relationship with him.

1. Take a few minutes to meditate on Psalm 119:71–80. Consider which thoughts or attitudes expressed by the psalmist you would like to make your own.

2. Hebrews 12:10–11 says, "Our fathers disciplined us for a little while as they thought best; but God disciplines us for our good, that we may share in his holiness. No discipline seems pleasant at the time, but painful. Later on, however, it produces a harvest of righteousness and peace for those who have been trained by it."

   If God is indeed sculpting each of us to make us more like Jesus Christ so that we can share in his holiness, how far along would you say you are in the process? In which areas of your life might God be disciplining you in order to make you more Christlike? How do you intend to respond to his discipline?

Personal Journey: To Do on Your Own

Set aside some time to do the following exercise.

1. The story of Job's trials and suffering, as recorded in the book of Job, provides insight into how God uses suffering to fulfill his plans—for us, for others, for his kingdom. Note the impact of Job's suffering even though he was unable to know what it all meant at the time.

What God Did	At first God allowed Satan to test Job but not to harm Job's body. Then, at Satan's request, God allowed Satan to afflict Job's body but not to kill him. • God gave permission for Satan's actions but didn't do them. • God put limitations on Satan's fury. • God allowed people to deliberately do evil and permitted the impersonal evil of bad storms. • God forced no one's hand, bypassed no one's will, and (from what we know) suspended no natural laws in allowing Job's suffering to occur. • When Satan had spent his fury against Job, God relieved Job's suffering, healed his disease, and showered him with blessing.
What Satan Did	Satan asked permission from God to stir things up. Acting freely, seeking to wreck Job's life and humiliate God, Satan engineered the carnage in Job's life

continued on next page . . .

What Happened to Job	• Evil brigands stole all of Job's donkeys, oxen, and camels and killed his servants and herdsmen; lightning killed all of Job's sheep and shepherds; a wind collapsed a house, killing all of Job's children. • When Job became diseased after losing all of his material wealth and children, friends came to comfort him, but also falsely accused him. • Job suffered greatly (even despairing of life) but remained faithful to God. His faithfulness resulted in God's winning a cosmic spiritual battle. In the end, God rewarded Job and praised Job's faith as an example to his friends.
What Was the Impact?	• Satan was defeated in a cosmic spiritual battle. • Job came to a greater realization of his own sin and came to know God in a way he never had before. • Job's friends also learned a thing or two about God. • Thousands of years after Job lived, his story is still teaching us about God and his relationship to our suffering.

2. Write a short, personal summary of some of the suffering you have experienced or perhaps are experiencing now. Then step back and try to view your suffering from God's broader perspective. Write a few sentences to describe the bigger picture you discover. If you aren't sure how to start, use the following questions as a guide:

- In what ways have I suffered? (Physically? Emotionally? Financially? Socially? Spiritually?)

- How might my suffering be accomplishing something God loves?

- In what ways might God be limiting the evil of what is happening to me?

- What might be at stake spiritually as a result of my suffering?

- In what ways have I grown in my relationship with God as a result of my suffering?

- In what ways has my suffering had an impact on other people?

- In what ways is my suffering like the suffering of Christ or making me more Christlike?

- How have I responded to my suffering? (My reactions and responses? My attitude toward God? My attitude and actions toward other people?)

- How might God want me to respond differently toward my suffering?

Session Three

How We Respond to Suffering Matters

Each day we go on living *means* something. God is up to something good when it comes to our trials. There are reasons. For us, for others, for the glory of God, and for the heavenly hosts.

—JONI EARECKSON TADA

Questions to Think About

1. When we suffer, what happens to us on the inside? How do we change? What do we think? How do we feel?

2. To what extent do you believe a person's view of God influences his or her response to suffering? Explain your answer.

3. If you knew for certain that your response to suffering made a difference in the unseen spiritual realm, how might your response be different?

4. When you know you will be facing a difficult day, how do you respond? How do you start the day?

Session Three: *How We Respond to Suffering Matters* • 45

Video Observations

A blessed start

Who do you live for?

Suffering shapes us into Christ's image

How we respond—it matters

Video Highlights

1. What do you think about what Joni describes as "the only way to start a day"? What possibilities does this perspective offer for your life?

2. First Peter 5:6–7, a passage highlighted in the video, says to "humble" ourselves before God. What does this mean, and what might be the link between our humility and God's ability to "lift us up" and care for us when we suffer?

Reflections of God's Glory

Through paralyzed hands I want to extend the grace of God and help people to say *no* to the worry and complaining and grumbling and self-centeredness—and *yes* to the grace of God. That ... promotes what real healing is all about. —JONI EARECKSON TADA

3. One recurring concept in this video, and this series, is that suffering helps shape us into the image of Jesus Christ. In what ways do you find it challenging to imagine that when you are suffering you are being shaped into the image of Christ? Or do you think it's easy? Be honest!

Large Group Exploration

Our Response to Suffering Has an Impact

In his Word, God gives us important, even surprising, insights into how our suffering can make a difference. God in heaven, for example, takes note of our suffering and the ways in which we invest ourselves in people's lives. The Bible clearly reveals that each of us has a part in carrying out God's plans—in the visible world as well as in the unseen spiritual realm. Even when someone is suffering alone and unnoticed, his or her response to suffering has an impact!

1. Just before Jesus ascended into heaven, he gave his final command to his disciples (and this includes Christians today). Read Acts 1:8 to find out what job Jesus wants his followers to do during their days on earth. In what ways does this command change when we suffer?

2. Philippians 1:25–26 reveals one kind of impact a Christian can have on other people. What is it?

3. According to Ephesians 3:8–11, what other significant impact do Christians have on the world around them? (See also Luke 15:10.)

4. The body of Christ includes Christians who experience suffering. Read the following Scripture passages and note the impact of those who suffer.

Scripture Passage	Impact of Those Who Suffer
1 Corinthians 1:27–31	
1 Corinthians 12:18–26	
2 Corinthians 1:3–5	
James 2:5	

Reflections of God's Glory

Nothing is lacking when it comes to what Christ did on the cross. It is finished, just as he said. But something is lacking when it comes to showcasing the salvation story to others. Jesus isn't around in the flesh, but you and I are. When we suffer and handle it with grace, we're like walking billboards advertising the positive way God works in the life of someone who suffers. —JONI EARECKSON TADA

5. What else—something that is exceedingly precious to God—can our response to suffering accomplish? (See Hebrews 13:15–16.)

> ### Reflections of God's Glory
>
> So many in our culture of comfort ... need the power of example. They need to see someone experiencing greater conflict than they *make it*. "We do not want you to become lazy, *but to imitate those* who through faith and patience inherit what has been promised" (Hebrews 6:12). —JONI EARECKSON TADA

Small Group Exploration

Sculpting Us into the Image of Christ

An artist once asked the great sculptor Michelangelo what he saw when he approached a block of marble. He replied, "I see a beautiful form trapped inside, and it is simply my responsibility to take my mallet and chisel and chip away until the figure is set free." In a similar way, God sees the beautiful form of Jesus Christ when he looks at our rough exterior. Just as a skilled sculptor uses a hammer and chisel to fashion a figure out of marble, God uses suffering to shape us into the image of Jesus Christ. Let's explore this truth together.

1. What is God trying to accomplish in our lives? What image does he have in mind? (See Romans 8:29; Ephesians 1:4.)

2. What are some of the practical results of the suffering God uses to conform us to the image of Christ? What does God require from us to accomplish his goal? (See Romans 5:3–5; Philippians 2:5–8, 12–15.)

3. Sometimes suffering people focus on the "hammer and chisel" and bemoan what God is chipping away. But the pain of God's chipping away produces something in us. Read the following passages. What are the process and result of what God is doing? In light of his intent, where should we place our focus?

   a. 2 Corinthians 3:7–18

   b. 2 Corinthians 4:7–11

4. The apostle Paul frequently taught about God's perfecting work in the life of the believer and often used himself as an example. What value does Paul see in his sufferings in 2 Corinthians 12:7–10?

5. What, according to the apostle John, is the key to having a fruitful life that impacts other people for Jesus Christ? (See John 15:5–8.)

> ### Reflections of God's Glory
>
> God's heart intent is to alleviate suffering.... He rallies us to his noble cause... longs to push back the pain through those who serve as his body, his hands and feet on earth. —JONI EARECKSON TADA

Group Discussion

1. Our initial response to suffering is often "Make it go away!" But in this session, we have further explored God's purpose in our suffering and considered how our responses to suffering can make a significant difference. In what ways, as a result of our exploration, are you able to see your suffering (or that of a loved one) in a different light? What possibilities for different (and hopefully better) responses to your suffering do you now see?

2. In what ways did the video footage of the Joni and Friends family retreat personalize what it means for members of Christ's body to help and encourage one another?

3. Since God has chosen those who are poor in the world's eyes to be rich in faith (James 2:5), what are some practical ways in which we can get closer to the "weaker" members of our fellowship and both honor and learn from them?

4. Think of people you personally know who have suffered. What impact did they have on you? What message about life and relationship with God did they communicate to the visible world and to the unseen spiritual realm?

Reflections of God's Glory

The test of suffering ... will always reveal the core of who we are. If we love ourselves selfishly, suffering will carbonate into sin. Evil in us will fizz to the surface and spread poison. Hardships will make us hateful and, in order to avoid suffering, we will inflict pain on ourselves and flail out at others. When that happens, suffering makes us worse than we were. Affliction doesn't teach us about ourselves from a textbook, it uses the stuff inside of us. —JONI EARECKSON TADA

Personal Journey: To Do Now

Spend a few minutes alone with God to consider how you view your suffering and how you could respond to it in ways that deepen your relationship with God.

1. Which of the following is happening in your life as a result of God's "hammering and chiseling"?

   ❏ Feeling confused; can't seem to figure out what God is doing
   ❏ Making clear decisions as a result of my relationship with God
   ❏ Believing that all things are working together for my good
   ❏ Trying to figure out how to escape my suffering at all costs
   ❏ Improving in my relationships—people matter more to me now
   ❏ Heaven is becoming more real to me, so I want to live a more godly life
   ❏ Spending more time with God—and enjoying it more
   ❏ Feeling angry at God right now and expressing it to him
   ❏ Being more aware of temptations—and with God's help standing more firmly against them
   ❏ Still trying to be in control of my life
   ❏ Feeling beaten down, in one sense, yet knowing God is at work in my life
   ❏ More confident than ever that God loves me and is shaping/using me for his glory
   ❏ More sensitive to hurting people
   ❏ Pretty self-focused right now but wishing things were different

- ❏ Reaching out to people more in order to share Jesus' love with them
- ❏ Learning to praise God in everything, including my suffering
- ❏ Inner qualities are developing more—patience, kindness, etc.
- ❏ More aware of my sin—and more willing to confess it to God
- ❏ Not wanting to trust God fully right now

2. I want my response to suffering to change in this way:

3. If asked to describe your response to suffering in your life (or the lives of people you love), what would the people who know you best say?

Personal Journey: To Do on Your Own

Set aside some time to do the following exercise.

1. In *When God Weeps,* Joni wrote, "Affliction either warms you up toward spiritual things or turns you cold.... lukewarmness is the only road that never gets to God.... Strong emotions open the door to asking the really hard questions.... Our deep emotions reveal the spiritual direction in which we are moving. Are we moving toward the Almighty or are we moving away from him?"

   Spend some time alone and consider your relationship with God in light of your suffering. What's the temperature of your relationship with God? Are you moving toward God or away from him? Is this the direction in which you want to be going? If not, what needs to change?

2. We can't fulfill God's purposes for our suffering if our relationship with him is broken. Ask God to reveal to you everything that may be hindering your relationship with him. Some common hindrances to an intimate relationship with God in the midst of suffering include:

   - Depending on ourselves and our own strength rather than on God

- Focusing on ourselves and our pain rather than on God and his work
- A lack of trust in God and his good character

You also may know of specific sins that stand between you and God.

To strengthen your relationship with God, consider your response to each of these hindrances. For which do you need to ask God's forgiveness? For which do you need to recognize your weakness and ask for his strength? For which do you need his help to conquer your unbelief? For which do you need to offer a sacrifice of praise? For which do you need to focus on God's holy, loving character?

3. Praise God for what he is doing in and through your life. Ask him to put hope in your heart and fill you up with his character and strength so that you will reflect his glory as you face the challenges of your life.

Session Four

Jesus Gives Us Hope

Suffering has no meaning in itself. Left to its own, it is a frustrating and bewildering burden. But given the context of relationship, suffering suddenly has meaning.... If I'm to be held steady in the midst of my suffering, I want to be held not by a doctrine or a cause but by the most powerful Person in the universe.

—JONI EARECKSON TADA

Questions to Think About

1. During a time of suffering, do you find it easier or harder to reach out to God? Why do you think that is?

2. What kind of things do you share with God concerning your suffering?

3. What do you think are the most important ingredients in cultivating an intimate relationship with God through Jesus Christ? What role do you think suffering plays in that relationship?

4. To what degree does what happened at the cross of Christ make a difference in your suffering today?

Video Observations

Things just don't go like Disneyland

Jesus: our one great hope, power, and solace

    Jesus is our fellow sufferer

    Jesus is our advocate with the Father

    We know Jesus by sharing in his sufferings

Video Highlights

1. Few people can share about their relationship with God with the convincing realism that Joni and Melanie conveyed through their comments. In what ways did their testimony make Christ's hope, solace, and inspiration more real to you? What have they experienced that touched a chord in your heart?

2. Why is it important for a person to have a personal relationship with God through Jesus Christ, as opposed to just knowing *about* Jesus? What does Jesus offer that is particularly significant when we face suffering?

3. Joni described being "swallowed up" by the suffering caused by her broken neck, which she views as God's way of pushing the "fast-forward button" on her life. What did she mean by this, and what was she desperate to find?

Large Group Exploration

The Victory of the Cross

Above all else, what Jesus accomplished on the cross pays the price for our sins and restores every believer's relationship with God. But the cleansing power of the cross also draws us into relationship with Jesus and empowers us to live a victorious life. Joni explained this in *When God Weeps,* where she wrote, "A miraculous exchange happens at the cross. When suffering forces us to our knees at the foot of Calvary, we die to self. We cannot kneel there for long without releasing our pride and anger, unclasping our dreams and desires—this is what 'coming to the cross' is all about. In exchange, God imparts power and implants new and lasting hope. We rise, renewed." Let's see what Scripture says about what the cross accomplishes in our daily lives.

1. What does 1 Corinthians 1:18 tell us about the message of the cross?

The Power of the Cross

Resurrection power is found at the cross, the place where we die to fierce unrest and low ambition. Resurrection power is cleansing power. Purifying power. It's the ability to sweep clean every skeleton in your closet and shake loose every monkey off your back. Strength to break the ball and chain around your soul and swing wide the prison door to the fresh air of freedom. Power to say no to doubts and fears and power to say yes to God's enabling. It's what 2 Timothy 2:11–12 is all about: "If we *die* with him, we shall also *live* with him; if we *suffer* with him, we shall also *reign* with him." ... Resurrection power is meant to uproot sin out of our lives. Then we, with holy hearts, experience a greater degree of his love. It is in Christ's love that we become more than conquerors.   —JONI EARECKSON TADA

2. In *When God Weeps,* Joni wrote, "The cross is the center of our relationship with Jesus. Something literal happened there 2,000 years ago. It is where we were given spiritual birth. Something symbolic is happening still: the cross is where we die." What does Colossians 3:1–10 say about this place of death? What kinds of things does God want us to die to?

3. According to Galatians 2:20 and Philippians 4:13, who helps us face our fears, negative emotions, and other potential sins?

> ### The Power of the Cross
>
> As time passes, the memory of our desperate state when we first believed fades. The cross was something that happened to us "back then." We forget how hungry for God we once were. We grow self-sufficient. We go through the motions—turning the other cheek and going the extra mile—but the effort is just that, an effort. We would hardly admit it, but we know full well how autonomous of God we operate. This is where God steps in. He permits suffering.... When suffering forces us to our knees at the foot of Calvary, we die to self.... Just when we begin to get a tad self-sufficient, suffering presses harder. And so, we seek the cross again.... God reveals more of his love, more of his power and peace as we hold fast the cross of suffering.... Deeper and more delightful, onward and upward we journey toward the cross, confessing and trusting, yielding and obeying.
>
> —JONI EARECKSON TADA

4. What does Christ's death on the cross lead us to do? Why? (See 2 Corinthians 5:14–15; 1 Peter 4:1–2.)

> ## The Power of the Cross
>
> When something marvelous happens between God and us, his cross no longer seems just a symbol of death. Another miraculous exchange occurs: the cross becomes a symbol of life. Victorious life. We no longer go to the cross kicking and screaming, we race to it for dear life. "The love of Christ compels us" to yield further to love's demands; thus we "throw off everything that hinders and the sin that so easily entangles" (2 Corinthians 5:14; Hebrews 12:1).
>
> —JONI EARECKSON TADA

Small Group Exploration

Intimacy Grows as We Share in Christ's Sufferings

"Intimacy happens as two souls rub together," Joni wrote. "It's what we long for more than anything else. To know and be known. Even in the best relationships, we are still left aching for someone to comprehend our world and enter our struggle—to embrace us with a passion that seizes and melts us into a union that will never be broken. God answers that ancient longing." He answers it by identifying with us in our suffering and by our identification with Christ's sufferings. As nothing else can, this sharing of suffering causes us to grow in intimacy with Christ. So let's consider how closely our hearts are linked to God's through suffering.

1. What did the apostle Paul pray that the Ephesian believers would experience? (See Ephesians 1:17–21.)

2. Jesus, our Lord and Savior, is well acquainted with our suffering. Not one bit of it escapes his notice. According to the following verses, how does he relate to our suffering?

    a. Acts 9:1–5

    b. Hebrews 4:15

THE POWER OF THE INCARNATION

Scripture reveals that Jesus, although he was fully God, shared in our humanity in every way (Hebrews 2:14–18). While on earth, he lived as a man, and like a man, he suffered. The prophet Isaiah revealed that Jesus "was despised and rejected by men, a man of sorrows, and familiar with suffering" (Isaiah 53:3). Let's consider some of the suffering that Jesus experienced, some of which is much like our own.

Verses	Suffering Jesus Experienced
Matthew 2:13–15	Lived as a refugee in Egypt
Matthew 2:16–18	Knew that his coming had caused the deaths of many baby boys in and around Bethlehem
Matthew 4:1–11	Was tempted by Satan after forty days and nights of fasting—one day for every year the Israelites wandered in the wilderness
Matthew 12:14; John 11:45–53	Jewish religious leaders plotted to kill him
John 7:12	Some people believed he was a deceiver
Mark 6:1–4	The people of his hometown rejected him
John 8:57–59; 10:31–39	At various times, people tried to stone him
Matthew 23:37–38	His heart ached over Jerusalem's terrible future
Matthew 26:36–40	Was overwhelmed with sorrow and loneliness in Gethsemane
Matthew 26:47–56	Was abandoned by all his disciples when the crowd came to him in Gethsemane
Matthew 26:60	Was accused by false witnesses during his trial
Matthew 26:67–68; 27:30–31	Despite his innocence, was spit on, struck with fists, slapped, beaten, and mocked
Matthew 27:32–35	Was crucified by Roman soldiers
Matthew 27:45–46	Was separated from God the Father because of the sin of the world that he bore for our sake

c. Hebrews 13:5–6

d. Psalm 68:19

3. What do the Scripture passages above help you remember about your relationship with Christ?

> ### The Power of the Incarnation
>
> When the Son of Man walked on earth, he had the comfort of his Father, but none from his friends.... He went without comfort so that you might be comforted. He went without joy so that you might have it. He willingly chose isolation so that you and I might never be alone. Most wonderfully, he bore God's wrath so that you wouldn't. God has no anger for you; only forgiveness, mercy, and grace.
>
> —JONI EARECKSON TADA

4. In chapter 3 of his letter to the Philippians, Paul wrote about what is most valuable to him. Philippians 3:10 concludes, "I want to know Christ and the power of his resurrection and the fellowship of sharing in his sufferings, becoming like him in his death."

   a. The word translated "fellowship" in the original text is *koinonia*—the experience of sharing something in common. Why would Paul want to share in Christ's sufferings, even his death?

   b. Why is "the power of his [Christ's] resurrection" so important as we think about what suffering can accomplish in our lives?

Group Discussion

1. What is your response to the passion with which the apostle Paul expressed his commitment to know Christ and participate fully in the life of Christ—even in his suffering and death?

2. In what ways has your view of the cross as a vital part of your daily life been influenced by our study today?

3. According to what we have studied in this session, how much of a difference does it make to have an intimate relationship with Jesus when we face suffering? What has been your experience with Jesus in relationship to suffering?

4. What hope have you gained (or has been strengthened) through our study in this session? What difference will that hope make as you face suffering in your life or in the life of someone close to you?

Personal Journey: To Do Now

Spend a few minutes alone with God to consider your relationship with him.

1. Who understands your suffering? What things are you able to share with that person that you don't, or can't, share with anyone else?

2. Describe a time when you have experienced intimacy with God—feeling known, loved, or a part of what he is about. What preceded or made possible that time of intimacy? What did that closeness with God produce in your heart and life?

3. After reflecting on the level of intimacy you have experienced with God, what will you commit to do in the days and weeks ahead in order to strengthen your relationship with him?

Personal Journey: To Do on Your Own

Set aside some time to do the following exercise.

1. Instead of going to the cross to receive God's power and hope, what do you sometimes do to try to keep yourself going and to keep hopelessness, fear, anger, despair, or other emotions at bay?

2. What is keeping you from giving all of yourself to Jesus—from running to the cross and asking him to fill you with his power and hope?

3. What hope for your suffering and pain do you long for Jesus to offer? Is it the kind of hope he promises, or is it a hope that is wrapped up in your own self-sufficiency and independence from God?

   Remember, Jesus wants to give us the hope that comes from being wrapped up in *his* life, from pressing our hearts tightly to his. If this hope seems foreign or unattainable to you, take time each day to meditate on Philippians 3:7–10. Paul's perspective will help tune your heart to the hope that an intimate relationship with our Lord provides.

Session Five

Finding Contentment

When it comes to contentment, God *must* be our aim.... If you only try to stave off discontentment, you will fail miserably. Unless you add the massive promise of superior happiness in God ... you'll still be restless.   —JONI EARECKSON TADA

Questions to Think About

1. What differences do you see between long-term and temporary suffering? In what ways do your responses to each type of suffering differ? Be specific.

2. Has your suffering ever pushed you to the point of anger? Have you expressed anger toward God during those times? How did you feel about expressing anger to God? Was it a good thing? Why or why not?

3. How would you describe the difference between contentment and resignation?

4. Describe someone you know who has handled long-term suffering well or in a way you admired. What was different about that person's response?

Session Five: *Finding Contentment* • 79

Video Observations

Pain that will not go away

Hope for broken hearts

God comes running

Contentment versus resignation

Video Highlights

1. How important is companionship or fellowship when we suffer? What are some of the hazards of suffering alone and the benefits of being able to share our suffering?

2. Who is the most important person with whom we need to share about our suffering? Why?

3. In what ways does resignation differ from contentment? What is the source of each?

Learn the Secret

Contentment is a sedate spirit that is able to keep quiet as it bears up under suffering. Paul understood how to live this way. He *learned* it. It meant acquiring skills. Understanding something and then practicing it. What did he understand? "I have *learned the secret of being content* in any and every situation, whether well fed or hungry, whether living in plenty or in want" (Philippians 4:12).

—JONI EARECKSON TADA

Large Group Exploration

Finding Contentment

God never intended us to live lives of resignation or to bitterly block out the ache of emotional and physical pain. He doesn't want us to merely survive; he wants us to be content. Contentment is a place of rest and strength where we are, as Paul expressed it, able to face sorrow and yet always rejoice. (See 2 Corinthians 6:10.) Contentment isn't a gift we receive so we can continue on our merry way. Contentment is something we seek after, something we learn, a quality we gain by choice. Let's see what the Bible says about gaining contentment.

1. The apostle Paul knew that we attain contentment by making choices that run contrary to our human nature. So in several of his epistles he emphasized the importance of seeking contentment.

    a. Read 2 Corinthians 12:8–10 and Philippians 4:11–13. What "secrets" of contentment does he reveal in these passages?

    b. In what ways have you found these "secrets" to be true in your life?

> ## The Mathematics of Contentment
>
> Paul's arithmetic for contentment was to subtract his earthly wants so that something of greater value could be attained: Christ's cause advanced throughout the world. —JONI EARECKSON TADA

2. According to Jeremiah 29:13, what must we do to find contentment in our relationship with God?

3. Joni has discovered that one way to foster contentment is to share Jesus' love with needy people who also face difficult circumstances. What does Philippians 2:3–8 say about this?

4. We know of many, many situations through which the apostle Paul suffered. What was his overarching focus and hope as he faced the trials of his life? How far was he willing for his contentment in Christ to take him? (See Philippians 1:12, 19–21).

5. What can we learn about contentment from the way in which Jesus handled his suffering? (See Hebrews 12:2–3.)

AIM FOR CONTENTMENT

When it comes to finding contentment, we need to do more than avoid the negatives such as wayward thoughts, bad-mouthing our circumstances, or comparing ourselves with others whose lives seem easier. We need to pursue a different path. We need to seek God with all our hearts and choose to make him our aim. Here's how:

Know Whom to Seek When We Suffer	Psalm 16:11	Know who holds the key to life. Know who gives joy.
Recognize the Purpose for Suffering	2 Corinthians 7:9–10	Suffering according to the will of God produces repentance without regret. That's contentment!
Choose to Suffer for the Right Purpose	Hebrews 11:25	Choose to suffer for the promised Christ rather than to enjoy the fleeting pleasures and treasures of earth. Choose to look forward to God's reward.
Come and Be Filled	Matthew 4:4; John 6:35	We need more than bread to live on; we need God's Word, which whets our appetite for Jesus, the Bread of Life. When we come to him, he fills us and satisfies us, making us content.
Focus on Our Destiny	Revelation 21:3–7	In heaven, God will wipe away our sorrows and tears, filling our hearts with complete satisfaction and overflowing joy.

Small Group Exploration

Emotions That Rob Us of Contentment

Deep emotions force us to face questions we would rather ignore. So some of us try not to feel. We may blanket our emotions with distractions or drugs—hardly a recipe for contentment. Others of us use anger like a shield (or a weapon) to distance ourselves from God and other people, but we can't find contentment when we're fighting the only one who can provide it. Still others of us pick up such an overwhelming load of worry that we lose sight of even the possibility of contentment.

TOPIC A: Anger

1. What does God say our earthly lives will be like? How does God want us to respond to it? (See Jeremiah 33:3; John 16:33.)

2. Instead of expressing our anger toward God, many of us try to put it behind us and go on. The problem is that unresolved anger continues to simmer in the background. We may regain a sense of hope for a time, but the unresolved anger will bubble to the surface again and again, snuffing out our hope each time. What happens to us when our hope is revived, then snuffed out? (See Proverbs 13:12.)

3. In *When God Weeps*, Joni wrote, "If emotions are the language of the soul, then the Book of Psalms gives us the grammar and syntax, teaching us how to wrestle, inviting us to question and vent anger in such a way as to move up and out of despair." Let's read Psalm 44:13–26.

   a. What emotions and opinions about God and life did the writer express?

   b. In what ways are these expressions similar to what we sometimes feel?

   c. How do you think God responds to such bold words? (See Psalm 34:15–18.)

4. Since God is listening and waiting for our cries for help, what does the psalmist urge us to do? (See Psalm 27:14.)

5. What do we need to remember about God when we become angry about our circumstances? (See Psalm 18:30–36.)

FOCUS ON ANGER

Ephesians 4:26 reveals that not all anger is sin. Some anger is harmful, but anger can also be constructive and beneficial when it pushes us to move in the right direction. Note the differences between destructive anger and constructive anger.

Destructive Anger	Constructive Anger
Demands immediate release and relief independently of God.	Expresses itself honestly to God.
Despises being vulnerable and helpless.	Admits to God feelings of vulnerability, helplessness, and frustration.
Relishes being in control.	Acknowledges God is in control.
Promises satisfaction but leaves us empty.	Draws us closer to God, who can fill us up.
Empties our hearts of hope so we stop caring and feeling.	Continues to pursue the hope God provides—that one day we will be rescued, redeemed, and filled with joy.
Creates sullen despair and despondency.	Allows us even in our despair to move toward the God who offers joy and real hope, and lets us see him as he really is (not how we want him to be).
Hardens our hearts.	Keeps our hearts soft as we seek after God, who wants to reveal himself to us and embrace us with his love.

Topic B: Worry

We don't have to look very far to find a number of things to worry about. Life is full of uncertainties. Not one of us knows what will happen tomorrow, next week, or next year. So worry is an easy trap to fall into, and it eats away at contentment. Perhaps that's why the Bible includes many cautions against worry and explains how to face worry head on.

1. In his Sermon on the Mount, Jesus addressed many important issues related to godly living. One of the practical issues he addressed was worry.

    a. Which fundamental truths about God and life did Jesus want his disciples to realize? (See Matthew 6:25–34.)

    b. What key difference between people who know God and those who do not did Jesus emphasize in verses 28–32?

    c. Which antidote to worry did Jesus provide in verse 33?

GOD MEETS THE NEEDS OF HIS PEOPLE

Scripture	How God Meets Our Needs
Psalm 121:1–4	God is our helper. He watches over us constantly.
Psalm 31:19	God stores up his goodness for those who fear him, who take refuge in him.
Isaiah 25:4	God is a refuge for the needy, a shelter from the storm, and shade from the heat.
1 Peter 5:7	God wants us to give him all our worries because he cares for us.
Isaiah 41:10	We don't have to be afraid. God is with us. We can count on him to strengthen and help us.
Proverbs 2:6–8	God guards the way of just people and protects the way of those who remain faithful to him.
Isaiah 40:11	God watches over us carefully, as a shepherd tends his flock. He keeps us close to his heart.
Psalm 37:23–24	If we obey God, he will uphold us.
Psalm 46:1	God is truly our refuge and strength. He is always with us when we face difficult times.
Isaiah 46:4	God will sustain us throughout our lives and rescue us when we need help.

2. When Jesus explained the parable of the sower and the seeds that fell on various types of ground, what important truth did he reveal about worry? (See Luke 8:14.)

3. What caution did the psalmist repeat in Psalm 37:1–8?

    a. What is the result of fretting or worrying? In what ways does this result surprise or concern you?

    b. Note the many verbs—designating the actions we are to take to counteract worry—that are in this passage. In what ways do you think these actions promote contentment?

4. Where does Psalm 91:1–6 tell us we can find rest when we are stressed-out, when we suffer from illness or threatening circumstances? How does this passage help you find contentment?

One Day at a Time

The enemy of contentment is worry. In Jesus' Sermon on the Mount, the phrase he repeated most often was, "Do not worry." The Lord was wise in repeating his warnings so many times. He knows the devastating effects of anxiety and how it can corrode faith like acid, robbing you of joy and stealing your hope. I'm sure this is why Jesus said in the same sermon, "Therefore do not worry about tomorrow, for tomorrow will worry about itself. Each day has enough trouble of its own" (Matthew 6:34). The secret of being content is to take one day at a time. Not five years or ten at a time, but one day.

—JONI EARECKSON TADA

Group Discussion

1. What are some of your discoveries about worry and anger and how they rob us of contentment?

2. In a short amount of time, we've highlighted the path of contentment. We've investigated what it is, how we find it, and how we avoid things that rob us of contentment. But suffering is painful, and it is just plain hard to be content when we hurt.

   a. In what ways have you been encouraged to seek contentment when you are suffering? Is it hard for you to do? What turns your heart toward peace with God when suffering threatens to overwhelm you? How do you maintain your focus on God, for example, when you have spent every shred of concentration just to get out of bed in the morning?

b. In what ways can we encourage a suffering brother or sister in Christ to walk toward contentment in the midst of pain? How can we encourage others with appropriate sensitivity and love?

Personal Journey: To Do Now

Spend a few minutes alone with God to consider where you are in your relationship with him and how you can have a greater level of contentment as you face the trials and challenges of your life.

1. It's far easier to talk about contentment than it is to be content, isn't it? For various reasons we worry. We doubt God's character. We become angry when things don't seem to be going our way. Now might be a good time to assess your level of contentment and your relationship with God. If you were to assign a numerical value from one to ten (ten being most content) to your present level of contentment, what would it be?

2. Evaluate the stability of your present level of contentment. How much does your level of contentment change when the pressure of suffering intensifies? When do you find it most difficult to be content? What does this tell you?

3. In what ways have you confused resignation and dutiful acceptance with genuine contentment? How has this affected your relationship with God?

4. What steps will you take in order to move toward God and discover more of the contentment he provides?

5. Even if it feels awkward, take a few minutes right now to talk to God about how you feel toward him.

Personal Journey: To Do on Your Own

Set aside some time to do the following exercise.

1. Psalm 37 is a beautiful hymn that speaks of hopes, trials, strength, weakness, fear, blamelessness, righteousness, and danger. It encompasses many messages of how to find true contentment in the midst of trials and suffering.

   Set aside time to meditate on this psalm at least three times, if possible, before the next session.

   As you read it, write down the images that are especially meaningful to you. For example, during one reading you may want to record the portions of the psalm that give you hope. Another time, record which actions you need to take to find contentment. Note the portions of the psalm that lead you to focus on God and your relationship with him.

2. In *When God Weeps*, Joni wrote about the importance of feeding our minds and hearts on things that bring contentment rather than those things that arouse unfulfilled desire and discontentment. Which choices in your life feed godly contentment? Which ones create discontentment and foster unmet desires or frustrations? (Be honest! And be patient with yourself. Some of these points may take time to discover.)

3. Ask God to reveal anything in your life that may be keeping you from finding contentment. Ask him to help you address the issues he reveals.

Session Six

A Look toward Heaven

If we had an easy life, we would soon forget that we are eternal creatures. But hell's splashover won't allow that. It persistently reminds us that something immense and cosmic is at stake—a heaven to be reached, a hell to be avoided.... Thus, it is only fitting that God should give us some sense of the stakes involved.... He does this by giving us foretastes of heaven in the joys we experience, and foretastes of hell in our suffering. —STEVE ESTES

Questions to Think About

1. As you go about your daily activities, how much thought do you give to heaven? How much thought do you think you should give to heaven, and how might such thinking influence your life?

2. Why do you think many people believe in the existence of heaven but dismiss hell as a myth?

3. Describe a time in your life when the knowledge of your eternal future seemed very real to you or made a difference in your life.

4. What do you think will be the best thing about heaven?

Video Observations

Suffering turns our hearts toward the future—toward heaven

Living with a passion for eternity

Prayer and the Bible—lifting our eyes heavenward

The fruit of suffering—a divine future with God

Video Highlights

1. What did you see in this video that broadened your understanding of what it means to live with a passion for future things, even when we are suffering?

2. Steve Estes said that he thinks about heaven every day, that heaven is what drives him. What do you think he meant by that comment?

3. Why is it important to use the opportunities God gives us every day to "invest" in our eternal reward?

4. What roles do prayer and Bible reading play in giving us a visionary glimpse of heaven?

Large Group Exploration

The Reality of Hell

Many people refer to their suffering as "hell on earth," and in a sense it is. The only reason suffering isn't worse is because God sets limits on the suffering he allows. But the Bible teaches that there is a hell *after* earth where suffering knows no bounds. Let's consider why hell exists and why our suffering in this life is merely a wake-up call to the harsh realities that people who reject Jesus as their Lord and Savior will experience for eternity.

1. In *When God Weeps,* Steve wrote, "God didn't make hell for people.... It's *unnatural* for humans to be there—as unnatural as our turning our backs on a Creator who loved us—as unseemly as our shrugging the Father's kind arm from our shoulders while caressing Eden's serpent coiled around our hearts. God takes no joy in sending anyone to eternal misery ... but in dozens of passages God warns that he will hurl everyone into that unthinkable pit who persists in challenging or ignoring him." So if God didn't create hell for people, why did he create it? (Read Matthew 25:41.)

2. What does the Bible say about human sinfulness—the reason we have earned and deserve a place in hell? (See Romans 3:10–12, 23.)

3. According to the following Scripture passages, what has God already done about sin, and what will he do about sin in the future?

   a. John 1:29; 3:16–18

> **DID YOU KNOW?**
> Jesus actually mentioned hell more frequently than he did heaven. The list below gives us an overview of what Jesus said about hell:
> - Hell is like the darkness outside where there is loneliness and fear rather than the warm fellowship of celebration and feasting. There will be weeping and gnashing of teeth. (See Matthew 8:11–12.)
> - People in hell will feel remorse for missed opportunities and be concerned for family and friends on earth. (See Luke 16:19–31.)
> - Hell will be physically and spiritually unbearable. (See Matthew 10:28; 13:49–50.)
> - Hell will be a horrible place of eternal fire where there is no relief from the pain. (See Matthew 18:8–9; 25:41, 46; Mark 9:43–48; Luke 16:22–24.)

b. 2 Thessalonians 1:8–9

c. Hebrews 10:26–31

4. Suffering, which reminds us of the cosmic battle between God and Satan, is a consequence of sin. In 2 Corinthians 4:16–18, what did Paul say our taste of a little bit of hell on earth accomplishes?

Small Group Exploration

A Look toward Heaven

So much of how we face suffering depends on our perspective, and the Bible repeatedly reminds us to live the present with our future clearly in view. For the Christian, the future gives us reason to hope. Every good pleasure on earth is but a shadow of its fulfillment in heaven. The hope of heaven can fill us with joy even when the present is filled with pain. A future vision also helps us choose to live according to eternal values rather than earthly values that will fall by the wayside. Let's take a few minutes to refresh our heavenly view.

1. Scripture tells us to rejoice in our sufferings! What do our sufferings accomplish for us? What do we have to look forward to because of what we suffer in this life? (See Romans 8:17–18.)

2. Read Colossians 3:1–4.

    a. On what does Paul remind us to focus our hearts and minds as we go through life?

Suffering Today for God's Eternal Kingdom

God is at work right now, building his kingdom. While on earth, Jesus began to reverse the effects of sin and its results—pain, death, and disease. But it was just a beginning. Today we still suffer, but God uses our suffering to draw people to himself. He is "patient ... not wanting anyone to perish, but everyone to come to repentance" (2 Peter 3:9). Paul realized that God—the God of love who wants to rescue every person's soul from hell—was using Paul's suffering to advance his kingdom. Eager to be with God in heaven, Paul bided his time patiently (Romans 8:23–25). Knowing that earth longed for God to finish his work, Paul wrote this about his suffering: "Now I want you to know, brothers, that what has happened to me [imprisonment] has really served to advance the gospel" (Philippians 1:12).

b. What is the significance of focusing our hearts and minds on the things of heaven?

c. What does God promise to those who "have been raised with Christ"?

> ## Just a Reminder!
>
> People whose hearts are ignited for heaven make good inhabitants of earth. —JONI EARECKSON TADA

3. According to Philippians 3:20–21, 1 Corinthians 13:12, and Revelation 21:3–4, what can we hope for in heaven?

4. When our suffering leaves us feeling isolated, out of sorts, like we just don't fit in here on earth, what comfort can we find in Philippians 3:20–21?

Group Discussion

1. Joni wrote, "God has every intention of rewarding your endurance.... Every tear you've cried—think of it—will be redeemed. God will give you indescribable glory for your grief.... The more faithful to God we are in the midst of our pain, the more our reward and joy." What difference does this truth make in light of your suffering or the suffering of someone you love? In what ways does it motivate or inspire you?

2. In what ways can God use our suffering here on earth to make an eternal impact on other people?

3. It's good to talk about suffering and its purpose, what it can accomplish in our lives, but what practical difference has suffering made (or should it make) in your life?

4. Describe the ways in which your view of suffering has changed since we began this study.

5. With which aspects of suffering that we have explored in this study do you struggle—to understand, to believe, to act upon? Why?

6. Describe a time when the "ice-cold splash of suffering" has awakened you from spiritual slumber and reminded you of heaven and/or hell.

Personal Journey

Spend a few minutes alone with God to consider what difference heaven makes in your daily life.

1. What difference does the future perspective we have explored in this session make in your life today?

    a. How does it change the way in which you suffer?

    b. How does it cause you to respond to people who are not yet Christians?

    c. How does it affect your relationship with God?

    d. How can you better accept your suffering, or that of a loved one, in light of an eternal future with God in heaven?

2. If you are suffering right now, focus your thoughts on the blessings God has provided. Thank him for those blessings and the foretaste he has given you of what's to come in heaven. Ask him to fill you with hope, peace, and joy because of what it will be like to be with him for eternity. Ask him to give you his power and strength to enable you to reflect his character to the watching world. And ask him to guide you to someone with whom you can share the gospel this week.

For More Information:

Joni Eareckson Tada
Joni and Friends
P.O. Box 3333
Agoura Hills, CA 91376
www. joniandfriends.org

When God Weeps

Why Our Sufferings Matter to the Almighty

JONI EARECKSON TADA AND STEVEN ESTES

If God is loving, why is there suffering?

After more than thirty years in a wheelchair, Joni Eareckson Tada's intimate experience with suffering gives her a special understanding of God's intentions for us in our pain. In *When God Weeps*, she and lifelong friend Steven Estes probe beyond glib answers that fail us in our time of deepest need. Instead, with firmness and compassion, they reveal a God big enough to understand our suffering, wise enough to allow it, and powerful enough to use it for a greater good than we can ever imagine.

Hardcover: 0-310-21186-7
Softcover: 0-310-23835-8

Also by Joni Eareckson Tada

A Step Further
Softcover: 0-310-23971-0

Heaven
Softcover: 0-310-21919-1

Diamonds in the Dust
Hardcover: 0-310-37950-4

More Precious Than Silver
Hardcover: 0-310-21627-3

Pick up a copy at your favorite bookstore!

GRAND RAPIDS, MICHIGAN 49530 USA
WWW.ZONDERVAN.COM